A Lamb Called Love

Author : Milly Bennitt-Young

Illustrator : Bishoy Gendi

Editor : Shereen Tadros

Produced by Seraph Creative

A Lamb Called Love

Text copyright © 2014 by Milly Bennitt-Young   Artwork copyright © 2014 Bishoy Gendi
Type-setting & Layout by FelineGraphics
All rights reserved. No part of this book, artwork included, may be used or reproduced in any matter without the written permission of the publisher.
ISBN 978-0-9946974-5-5   Copyright © 2014 Seraph Creative

Authors note

A Lamb called Love is a funky retelling of creation and the gospel. I hope this book will break in pieces any thought that God can be confined to a box of our understanding.

It was written following a vision that I had while living in Hong Kong. I was filled with wonder at God's love and grace towards me and how that empowers us to participate with heaven. This revelation sparked a desire to invite future generations of world changers into the fun adventure of tangible relationship with the Trinity, established in the security of knowing Love.

It has been great to work with Bishoy who has marvellously captured the extravagance and wonder of the Trinity.

I hope you enjoy and participate in the adventure as you read,

Milly

A Lamb Called Love

Before time and hours and the stars above
Papa and Spirit were singing with Love

Although it was dark like the blackest night
Their beautiful chorus switched on the light.

Together they made the rivers and sky
The mountains and forests, the birds that fly

But Man was the only one who was like them
Papa's true masterpiece, Love's greatest gem.

They showed Man the beasts
— the big and the small

With Papa beside him,
he named them all.

Then, while he slept,
         they made from his side

A Woman to love
       — an equal; a bride.

Woman and Man were so happy and glad
Best friends with Papa, they never felt sad.

Then Snake came along and whispered his lie
He wanted Man and the Woman to die.

When they believed him, they thought all was lost
But Love made things right despite the great cost.

The Lamb we call Love died for you and me
To give us new hearts and new eyes to see.

Spirit breathed in Love

restored him to life

So we could be free

from sorrow and strife.

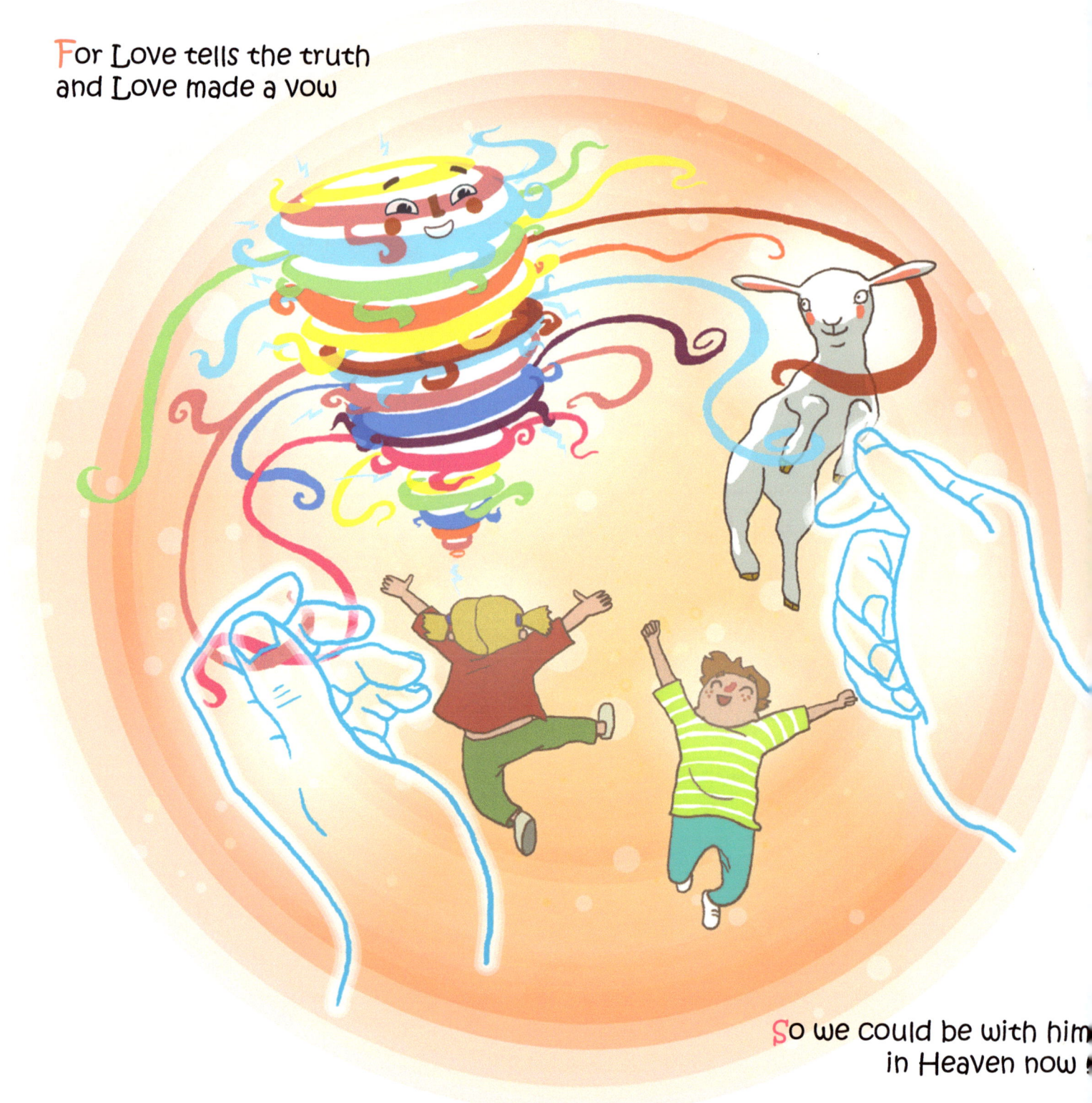

Love gave us power,
now Snake has to flee

He's a weakling compared
to you and me!

Love keeps in a bottle
 your precious tears
He takes away worries
 and chases fears.

And still they are singing their happy song
A song that reminds us where we belong

A song so beautiful, merry and wild......

"Always remember,
I love you my child"

A Lamb Called Love

Milly Bennitt-Young

Milly currently lives in the south of England. She has lived all over the world sharing the love of God.

Milly enjoys daily encounters with God in heaven and on the earth. She hopes to give children the inspiration to step into the reality of heaven. That they would feel empowered, loved by a fun God with an open invitation to experience Him in all His fullness and to grow in their journey walking in the ways of Love.

You can follow Milly and her journey at
www.cabinacademy.com

Bishoy Gendi

Bishoy is an illustrator and animator living and working in London who loves to make stories and characters come to life. He has a gorgeous wife and three beautiful little girls.

You can follow Bishoy at
www.bishoygendi.blogspot.com

Seraph Creative

Seraph Creative is a collective of artists, writers, theologians & illustrators who desire to see the body of Christ grow into full maturity, walking in their inheritance as Sons Of God on the Earth.

You can contact us or check out our latest resources at
www.seraphcreative.org

Note from the Publisher:

"A Lamb Called Love" is quite a book. Received in a vision in Sai Kung, Hong Kong; completed in Sydney, Australia; illustrated in London, England; formatted on the Island of Patmos, Greece (of Revelations fame) and the ancient city of Smyrna, Turkey (also of Revelations fame), formatted for print in Cape Town, South Africa and finally converted to eBook in Arizona, USA.

It is a privilege to be involved with Milly and Bishoy and we hope to see much more. We know "A Lamb Called Love" will open you and your children even further to the Love and reality of the Trinity.

NOW AVAILABLE IN eBOOK

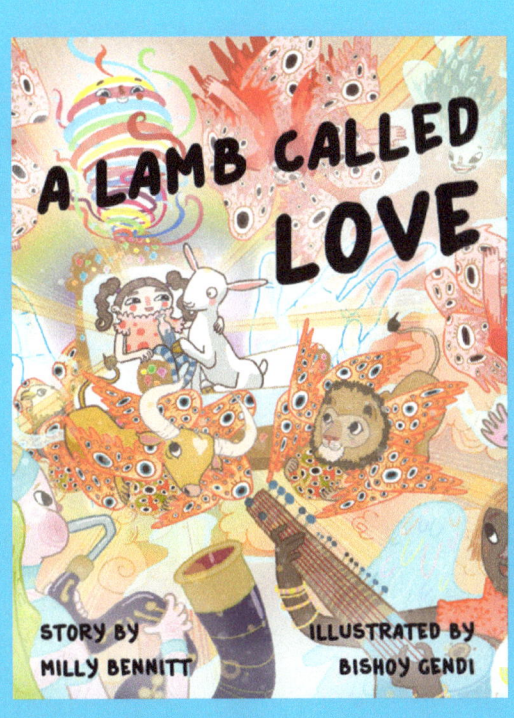

Apple iBooks
(with author
read-a-long)
Amazon Kindle
and any device with
Amazon Kindle
applications.

See our website for more amazing children's books and eBooks

seraphcreative.org

www.ingramcontent.com/pod-product-compliance
Lightning Source LLC
Chambersburg PA
CBHW040731150426
42811CB00063B/1573

9780994697455